My Journey Through Life:
A Personal Memoir

Jim Stephens

Published by RWG Publishing, 2023.

Table of Contents

Chapter 1: The Beginning: My Childhood and Early Years

The first memories of my life are of a small, cozy home filled with the love and laughter of my family. I was the youngest of three children, and my parents doted on me constantly. My childhood was one of simplicity and innocence, filled with the joys and wonders of discovery.

I grew up in a small town, surrounded by nature and the beauty of the countryside. My family was not wealthy, but we were happy and content with what we had. We spent most of our time outdoors, exploring the woods and fields around our home. I was always fascinated by the creatures and plants that we encountered, and I spent many hours studying and observing them.

My parents were my first teachers, and they instilled in me a love of learning and a curiosity about the world. They encouraged me to read and explore, and they were always willing to answer my questions. I was an inquisitive child, and I was always eager to learn more about the world around me.

As I grew older, I began to discover my own interests and passions. I loved to read, and I spent hours devouring books of all kinds. I was also interested in science and technology, and I spent many hours tinkering with gadgets and machines. I was always eager to learn more about how things worked, and I was always looking for new challenges and adventures.

My childhood was not without its struggles and hardships. I faced my fair share of bullies and mean-spirited classmates, and I sometimes felt like an outsider. But through it all, my family was always there to support and encourage me. They taught me to be strong and resilient, and they helped me to see the beauty and potential in myself.

Looking back on my childhood and early years, I realize how fortunate I was to have such a loving and supportive family. They shaped the person I am today, and I am forever grateful for the lessons and experiences they shared with me. My childhood was the foundation of my journey through life, and I will always cherish the memories of those early years.

Chapter 2: Discovering My Passion: My Journey to Finding Purpose

As I entered my teenage years, I began to realize that I needed to find my own path in life. I had always been a curious and ambitious person, but I wasn't sure what I wanted to do with my life. I knew that I wanted to make a difference and leave a lasting impact on the world, but I wasn't sure how to achieve that.

I experimented with different hobbies and interests, trying to find something that resonated with me. I tried my hand at music, art, and sports, but nothing seemed to click. I was beginning to feel lost and directionless, unsure of what my purpose in life was.

It wasn't until I was in college that I finally discovered my passion. I had always been interested in science and technology, but it wasn't until I took a class on environmental science that I realized how much I wanted to make a difference in the world. I became fascinated with the idea of using science and technology to solve environmental problems, and I knew that this was what I wanted to do with my life.

I threw myself into my studies, taking every class and opportunity that I could to gain more knowledge and skills. I researched and wrote papers on various environmental issues, and I participated in various projects and initiatives to raise awareness about the importance of sustainability. I was finally beginning to find my purpose and direction in life.

It wasn't an easy journey, and there were times when I doubted myself and my abilities. But I knew that this was what I was meant to do, and I was determined to make a difference. I graduated from college with a degree in environmental science, and I began my career as an environmental consultant. I knew that this was just the beginning of my journey, and I was excited to see what the future held.

Discovering my passion was a long and difficult journey, but it

was also one of the most
rewarding experiences of my life.
I finally had a sense of purpose
and direction, and I was eager to
make a difference in the world. I
knew that I had a long road ahead
of me, but I was ready for the
challenge.

Chapter 3: Leaving Home: My First Steps into Adulthood

Leaving home was one of the most difficult decisions I ever had to make, but it was also one of the most liberating. I had spent my entire life in the small town where I grew up, and I had always been surrounded by the love and support of my family and friends. But as I graduated from college, I realized that it was time for me to spread my wings and explore the world.

The decision to leave home was not an easy one. I was leaving behind everything that was familiar and comfortable to me, and I was stepping into the unknown. I was excited about the prospect of starting a new chapter in my life, but I was also scared and uncertain.

As I packed my belongings and said goodbye to my family and friends, I felt a mix of emotions. I was sad to be leaving the people and places that I loved, but I was also excited about the opportunities and experiences that lay ahead. I knew that I was about to embark on a journey that would change my life forever.

My first steps into adulthood were filled with challenges and struggles. I had to learn how to live on my own, how to budget my money, and how to navigate the complexities of the adult world. I had to learn how to make new friends and build a new support system. It was a difficult and often overwhelming process, but I knew that I was strong enough to handle it.

As I settled into my new life, I began to realize that leaving home was the best decision I ever made. I was surrounded by new and exciting opportunities, and I was finally living my life on my own terms. I was no longer a child, but a young adult who was in control of her own destiny. I was learning new things, meeting new people and exploring new places.

Leaving home was a turning point in my life, and it was the first step towards becoming the person I am today. It was a challenging and difficult process, but it was also a journey of self-discovery and growth. I am forever grateful for the lessons and experiences that I gained from leaving home and stepping into adulthood.

Chapter 4: Love and Loss: My Experiences with Relationships

Love and relationships have played a significant role in my life, and I have had my fair share of both joys and heartbreaks. I have learned that love is a powerful and complex emotion, and it can bring both happiness and pain.

I have had several relationships throughout my life, and each one has taught me valuable lessons. My first serious relationship was in college, and it was a time of discovery and growth. We were young and in love, and we were both excited about the future. But as time passed, we began to realize that we had different goals and aspirations, and we eventually grew apart. It was a difficult and painful experience, but it taught me the importance of being true to myself and finding someone who supports and complements me.

I had several other relationships after that, and I learned to be more cautious and selective about who I let into my heart. I had a few relationships that were filled with love and happiness, but I also had some that were filled with pain and disappointment. Each one taught me something new about myself and about relationships, and I began to realize that love is not always easy, but it is always worth it.

My most significant relationship was one that lasted for several years, and it was the one that I thought would last forever. We had built a life together and we had plans for the future. However, fate had other plans and we ended up separating. That was one of the most difficult and painful experiences of my life, and it took me a long time to heal and move on.

But through it all, I have learned that love is a journey. It's not always easy, and it's not always perfect. But it's always worth it. I've learned that relationships are not about finding someone who completes you, but finding someone who complements you, and who is willing to grow and evolve together.

Love and loss have been an integral part of my journey, and I have learned that love is not always a destination, but a journey. And I'm willing to continue traveling the path of love, the good and the bad, in the hope of finding someone special.

Chapter 5: Career and Success: My Professional Journey

My career has been a significant part of my journey through life, and I have worked hard to achieve my goals and aspirations. I've always been ambitious and driven, and I have always known that I wanted to make a difference in the world.

After graduating from college with a degree in environmental science, I began my career as an environmental consultant. It was a challenging and rewarding experience, and I was able to make a real impact on the world around me. I worked with a variety of clients, from small businesses to large corporations, and I helped them to reduce their environmental impact and become more sustainable.

I quickly realized that I had a talent for problem-solving and strategy, and I began to take on more responsibility within the company. I was promoted to a management position and soon I was leading a team of consultants. I enjoyed the challenges and the opportunity to make a difference.

However, as time passed, I began to realize that my passion for environmental science was not enough to fulfill my ambition. I wanted to make a larger impact and have more control over the direction of my career. So, I decided to pursue an MBA in order to gain the knowledge and skills I needed to take the next step in my career.

After completing my MBA, I landed a job in a top consulting firm, where I was able to apply my knowledge and skills to a wider range of projects and clients. I was able to make a real impact in the world of business and management, and I was quickly recognized as a rising star in the industry.

As I look back on my professional journey, I am proud of the accomplishments and the impact I have made. I have worked hard to achieve my goals, and I have been rewarded with a successful and fulfilling career. But I know that my journey is not over, and I am always looking for new challenges

and opportunities to grow and
make a difference in the world.

Chapter 6: Overcoming Obstacles: My Struggles and Triumphs

Life is not always easy, and I have faced my fair share of obstacles and challenges throughout my journey. But I have also learned that it is through these struggles that we grow and become stronger.

One of the biggest obstacles I faced was when I lost my job during the financial crisis of 2008. I had just finished my MBA and I was starting to establish my career, but the company I was working for went bankrupt and I found myself out of a job. It was a difficult and uncertain time, and I felt like my future was in jeopardy. But I knew that I couldn't give up and I had to keep moving forward.

I spent months searching for a job and going through interviews, but I was met with rejection after rejection. I felt like I had hit rock bottom, and I began to doubt my abilities and my worth. But I knew that I couldn't let this defeat me, and I decided to take control of my own future.

I decided to start my own consulting business, and I focused on using my skills and knowledge to help small businesses and entrepreneurs. It was a risky move, but it was also an opportunity to be my own boss and create my own path.

It was not an easy journey, and there were times when I wondered if I had made a mistake. But I was determined to make my business a success, and I put all my effort and dedication into it. Slowly but surely, my business began to grow, and I was able to make a difference in the lives of my clients and in my own life.

Overcoming this obstacle was one of the most difficult and challenging experiences of my life, but it was also one of the most rewarding. It taught me the importance of resilience, determination, and self-belief. I learned that when we are faced with adversity, we have the power to choose our own destiny.

Throughout my journey, I have faced many obstacles and challenges, but I have also learned that it is through these struggles that we grow and become stronger. I've learned that it's not about avoiding obstacles, but about facing them head-on and coming out victorious.

Chapter 7: Travels and Adventures: My Explorations of the World

Traveling and adventure have been a constant companion throughout my journey, and I have always been fascinated by the beauty and diversity of the world. I have had the privilege of visiting many different countries and cultures, and each experience has been unique and rewarding.

I have always been interested in exploring new places, and I have always been willing to step outside my comfort zone. I was always eager to learn about new cultures and ways of life, and I was always looking for new adventures and experiences.

One of my most memorable travels was when I visited Africa. I was able to see the wildlife and beautiful landscapes of different countries, and it was truly an unforgettable experience. I was also able to visit local communities and learn about their way of life and culture. It was a humbling and enlightening experience, and it helped me to appreciate the diversity and beauty of the world.

I have also been fortunate to travel to many different parts of Asia, including India, China, and Japan. Each country had its own unique culture and history, and I was able to learn about their customs and traditions. I also got to try different types of food and witness different festivals and ceremonies.

I have also traveled to Europe, where I was able to visit many different cities and countries, including Paris, Rome, and London. Each city had its own unique charm and character, and I was able to explore their rich history and culture. I was also able to experience different styles of architecture, art, and music.

Throughout my travels, I have learned that the world is a vast and wonderful place, and there is always something new to discover. I have also learned that the world is full of kind and friendly people, and that we are all connected by our shared humanity.

Traveling and adventure have been a constant companion throughout my journey, and I am forever grateful for the experiences and memories that I have gained. I know that there is still so much more of the world to explore, and I am excited to see what new adventures the future holds.

Chapter 8: Finding Faith: My Spiritual Journey

Faith and spirituality have always been an important part of my life, and I have always been searching for a deeper understanding of the world and my place in it. My journey to find faith has been a long and winding one, but it has been one of the most rewarding experiences of my life.

Growing up, I was raised in a religious household, and I was taught the basics of my faith. However, as I grew older, I began to question the beliefs and practices that I had been taught. I was searching for something deeper and more meaningful, and I was not finding it in the traditional religious practices that I had been exposed to.

I began to explore different spiritual paths and practices, looking for something that resonated with me. I tried meditation, yoga, and various forms of spiritual healing, and I found that they helped me to connect with something deeper within myself.

It was not until I took a trip to India that I truly began to understand the power and beauty of faith. I was exposed to a variety of spiritual practices and beliefs, and I was able to see how they helped people to connect with something greater than themselves. I was able to see how faith and spirituality could bring people together and help them to find peace and happiness in their lives.

After returning from India, I began to incorporate some of the spiritual practices that I had learned into my own life. I began to meditate regularly, and I found that it helped me to find inner peace and clarity. I also began to study different spiritual texts, and I found that they helped me to understand the world and my place in it.

Finding faith has been a long and winding journey, but it has been one of the most rewarding experiences of my life. I have learned that faith is not about following a set of rules or beliefs, but about finding a connection to something greater than ourselves. I have learned that faith is about finding peace and meaning in our lives, and about connecting with something that is greater than ourselves.

Chapter 9: Family and Friendship: My Support System

Family and friendship have been a constant source of support and guidance throughout my journey, and I am forever grateful for the love and care that they have provided.

My family has always been my rock, and I have always known that I could count on them for love and support. My parents taught me the values of hard work, perseverance, and compassion, and they have always been there to guide me and encourage me. My siblings have also been a constant source of support and inspiration, and I have always been grateful for the bond that we share.

My friends have also been a vital part of my journey, and I have been blessed to have a group of loyal and supportive friends. They have been there for me through the highs and lows, and they have always been willing to lend a listening ear or a helping hand. They have also been a source of laughter and joy, and I have always been grateful for the memories and experiences that we have shared.

I have also been fortunate to have mentors and role models in my life, who have helped me to grow and develop. They have been a source of guidance and inspiration, and I have always been grateful for the wisdom and advice that they have shared.

Family and friendship have been
an integral part of my journey, and
I have learned that the love and
support of others is essential for
our growth and well-being.

Chapter 10: Facing Fears: My Growth and Self-Discovery

Facing my fears has been a crucial part of my journey, and it has helped me to grow and discover more about myself. I have learned that fear is a natural part of life, and it is something that we all have to face at some point.

One of my biggest fears was public speaking. I have always been a shy and introverted person, and the thought of speaking in front of a large audience filled me with anxiety and dread. But I knew that if I wanted to succeed in my career, I had to overcome this

fear. So, I began to take small
steps to face my fear, such as
speaking in front of small groups
and gradually building up to larger
audiences.

I also faced my fear of failure. I
have always been a perfectionist
and I have always been afraid of
making mistakes. But I have
learned that failure is a natural part
of life, and it is through failure
that we learn and grow. So, I
began to take risks and try new
things, even if there was a chance
that I might fail. And I have
learned that failure is not the end,
but rather an opportunity to learn
and improve.

I have also faced my fear of change. I have always been a creature of habit, and I have always been afraid of stepping out of my comfort zone. But I have learned that change is necessary for growth, and that it is through change that we learn and discover more about ourselves. So, I began to embrace change and be open to new experiences and opportunities.

Facing my fears has also helped me to discover more about myself. I have learned that I am capable of more than I ever thought possible. I have learned that I am stronger and more resilient than I ever thought possible. I have also learned that I am more adaptable and open-minded than I ever thought possible.

Facing my fears has not been easy, and it has been a journey of self-discovery. I have learned that fear is a natural part of life and that it is through facing our fears that we grow and discover more about ourselves. I have learned that fear is not something to be feared, but something to be embraced, and that it is through facing our fears that we can break through our limitations and achieve our true potential.

Facing my fears has been a challenging and difficult process, but it has also been one of the most rewarding experiences of my life. It has helped me to grow and discover more about myself, and it has helped me to live a more authentic and fulfilling life. I will continue to face my fears and to push beyond my limits, knowing that this is what helps me to grow and evolve as a person.

Chapter 11: Making a Difference: My Contributions to Society

Making a difference in the world has always been a goal of mine, and I have always been driven to use my talents and resources to make a positive impact on society. I believe that each one of us has a responsibility to give back to the world and make a difference in the lives of others.

Throughout my career, I have been fortunate to work on projects that have had a direct and positive impact on society. I have worked on environmental conservation projects, which helped to protect natural habitats and preserve endangered species. I have also worked on poverty reduction programs, which helped to improve the lives of people living in underprivileged communities.

I have also been actively involved in volunteering and community service. I have volunteered with various organizations, such as shelters, schools, and hospitals. I have also been involved in fundraising campaigns for different causes, such as disaster relief and cancer research.

In addition to my professional and volunteer work, I have also been committed to living a sustainable lifestyle and spreading awareness about environmental conservation. I believe that it is important to take responsibility for our actions and make a conscious effort to reduce our impact on the environment.

Making a difference in society is not always easy, and it requires effort and dedication. But I have learned that every small action counts, and that together, we can make a significant impact. I have also learned that it is not about the magnitude of our contributions, but about the intention and the impact that we make.

Making a difference in society has been a fulfilling and rewarding experience, and I am proud of the contributions that I have made. I will continue to strive to make a positive impact on the world and to use my talents and resources to make a difference in the lives of others.

Chapter 12: Reflections: My Lessons Learned

As I look back on my journey, I am filled with gratitude and humility. I have been blessed with so many experiences and opportunities, and I have learned so many valuable lessons along the way.

One of the most important lessons that I have learned is the power of perseverance. I have learned that life is not always easy, and that there will be obstacles and challenges that we will have to face. But I have also learned that it is through perseverance and determination that we overcome these obstacles and achieve our goals.

I have also learned the importance of self-awareness and self-acceptance. I have learned that it is important to know ourselves and to accept ourselves for who we are. I have learned that when we are true to ourselves, we are able to live a more authentic and fulfilling life.

I have also learned the importance of relationships and connections. I have learned that the love and support of others is essential for our growth and well-being. I have learned that it is through our relationships and connections that we are able to find meaning and purpose in our lives.

I have also learned the importance of gratitude and perspective. I have learned that it is important to be grateful for what we have and to appreciate the small things in life. I have learned that when we have a positive perspective, we are able to find hope and joy in even the toughest of situations.

As I reflect on my journey, I am filled with gratitude and humility. I am grateful for the lessons that I have learned, and I am humbled by the experiences and opportunities that I have been given. I know that my journey is not over, and I am excited to see what new lessons and experiences the future holds.

Chapter 13: The Future: My Hopes and Dreams

As I look towards the future, I am filled with hope and excitement. I have accomplished so much in my journey so far, but I know that there is still so much more to achieve and experience.

One of my biggest hopes for the future is to continue making a difference in the world. I want to use my talents, resources, and experience to make a positive impact on society and to help improve the lives of others. I want to continue to work on projects that make a difference, whether it's in the field of environmental conservation, poverty reduction, or community service.

I also hope to continue my personal growth and development. I want to continue to challenge myself and push beyond my limits, whether it's through travel, education, or personal projects. I want to continue to learn and grow as a person, and to live a life that is true to myself.

I also hope to continue to build and strengthen my relationships. I want to continue to cherish and nurture the relationships that I have, and to make new connections with people from all walks of life. I want to continue to find joy and meaning in the love and support of others.

Finally, I hope to continue to find balance and happiness in my life. I want to continue to find peace and contentment in the present moment, and to find joy in the simple things in life.

As I look towards the future, I am filled with hope and excitement. I know that my journey is not over, and I am excited to see what new adventures and experiences the future holds. I am eager to continue to make a difference in the world and to live a life that is true to myself, with the love and support of my loved ones.

Chapter 14: Epilogue: My Legacy and Final Thoughts

As I come to the end of this journey, I am filled with a sense of accomplishment and gratitude. I have shared my experiences and reflections, and I have shared the lessons that I have learned along the way.

As I look back on my journey, I am proud of the contributions that I have made, both to society and to my own personal growth and development. I have worked hard to make a difference in the world, and I have tried to live a life that is true to myself. I have also been blessed with a loving family, supportive friends, and a wealth of experiences and opportunities.

As I look towards the future, I am filled with hope and excitement. I know that my journey is not over, and that there is still so much more to achieve and experience. I look forward to continuing to make a difference in the world, and to continue to learn and grow as a person.

As I leave behind my legacy, I hope that my story will inspire others to live their own journey with passion and purpose. I hope that my story will encourage others to face their fears, to pursue their dreams, and to make a difference in the world.

In conclusion, I want to express my gratitude to everyone who has been a part of my journey and has supported me throughout. To my

family, friends, and loved ones,
thank you for your love and
support. To my readers, thank you
for taking the time to read my
memoir and for sharing this
journey with me.

As I come to the end of my
journey, I am filled with a sense of
accomplishment and gratitude. I
am proud of the person I have
become and the experiences that I
have had, and I am excited for
what the future holds. This
journey has been a privilege, and I
am grateful for every step I've
taken.

Chapter 15: Appendix: My Letters and Other Memories

As I reflect on my journey, I am reminded of the many memories and keepsakes that I have collected along the way. In this appendix, I would like to share some of my most cherished memories and keepsakes, including letters, photographs, and other mementos that have helped to capture my journey.

One of the most meaningful keepsakes that I have is a collection of letters that I have received over the years. These letters have come from family, friends, and loved ones, and they have helped to capture the moments of my journey. They have been a source of support and encouragement, and they have helped to remind me of the love and care that I have been blessed with.

Another cherished keepsake that I have is a collection of photographs. These photographs have captured my experiences and adventures, and they have helped to remind me of the memories that I have made. They have also helped to capture the beauty of the world and the people that I have met along the way.

I also have a collection of other mementos that have helped to capture my journey. This includes souvenirs from my travels, such as postcards, trinkets, and other items that I have collected along the

way. These mementos have helped
to remind me of the experiences
and adventures that I have had,
and they have helped to capture
the memories of my journey.

In conclusion, this appendix is a
collection of my most cherished
memories and keepsakes that have
helped to capture my journey.
These letters, photographs, and
other mementos have been a
source of support and
encouragement, and they have
helped to remind me of the love
and care that I have been blessed
with. They have also helped to
capture the beauty of the world
and the experiences that I have
had along the way. They will
always be a reminder of my

journey, and I will always treasure them.